TRAIN THE TRAINER EXCELLENCE

GUIDE FOR SUCCESSFUL "TRAIN THE TRAINER"

SOWMYA NATARAJAN

Made with ♥ on the Notion Press Platform
www.notionpress.com

Train the Trainer Excellence

A Guide to Train the Trainer Success

Ms. Jacqueline Sowmya Natarajan

Assistant Professor & Soft Skills Trainer

Communication & Soft Skills Department

Koneru Koneru Lakshmaiah University, Vijayawada campus.

Contents

Preface

"To all aspiring trainers,

Welcome to the rewarding world of guiding others towards their full potential. As you embark on this journey, remember that being a trainer isn't just about imparting knowledge; it's about igniting inspiration, fostering growth, and cultivating lasting change.

May this book be your trusted companion, offering insights, strategies, and tools to hone your craft and empower those you teach. Embrace the opportunity to make a difference, to spark curiosity, and to fuel the flames of learning in others.

May your passion for training be contagious, your dedication unwavering, and your impact profound. Here's to the transformative power of education and the countless lives you'll touch along the way.

Whether you're a seasoned professional or just beginning your journey, this book offers valuable insights and practical advice to help you thrive in your role as a trainer.

In Chapter 1, "Introduction," we delve into the foundational aspects of becoming a professional trainer, exploring the goals and standards that define excellence in this field.

Chapter 2, "Five Hats of a Trainer," examines the multifaceted roles that trainers play, from being a professional and a medium of knowledge transfer to serving as a facilitator, teacher, and friend/mentor.

Chapter 3, "Activities Suiting the Learning Styles," focuses on understanding and catering to the diverse learning preferences of individuals, offering practical activities tailored to different learning styles.

In Chapter 4, "Interview of a Trainer," we gain insights into various training methodologies, delivery techniques, learning tools, and discipline handling strategies through an interview format.

Chapter 5, "TNA Form," introduces the concept of Training Needs Analysis (TNA) and emphasizes the importance of feedback in the training process.

Chapter 6 provides a detailed lesson plan on building confidence, a crucial skill for both trainers and learners alike.

Chapter 7, "Voice and Accent," delves into phonology and various aspects of pronunciation, offering guidance on improving vocal clarity and accent neutralization.

Lastly, Chapter 8 addresses student management strategies, essential for maintaining a conducive learning environment and fostering student engagement and success.

Throughout this book, you'll find practical tips, real-life examples, and actionable strategies aimed at enhancing your effectiveness as a trainer. Whether you're conducting workshops, delivering presentations, or facilitating group discussions, may this book serve as your trusted companion on your journey towards excellence in training.

ACKNOWLEDGEMENTS

I take this opportunity to express my profound gratitude and deep regards to my leaders and mentors for exemplary guidance, monitoring and constant encouragement throughout my work experience in various organizations. The advice and guidance given by them from time to time did carry me a long way in the journey of life on which I am grateful for.

I also take this opportunity to express a deep sense of gratitude to my husband, **Suresh Natarajan**, for his cordial support, valuable information and guidance, which helped me in completing this material through various stages.

I am thankful to my daughter, **Sheryl Blessy**, for the valuable support and encouragement during the making of my book.

Lastly, I thank Almighty God, my family and friends for their constant encouragement for making this book possible.

CONTENT

Table of Contents

I

INTRODUCTION

1.1 **BECOMING A PROFESSIONAL TRAINER**

The training field can change fast. New methodologies, new discoveries about the way adults learn, changing expectations from trainees demands this change. So the trainers need to get the practical platform skills and confidence they need to succeed. This project work puts the latest trends and techniques. Whether a trainer has been training for a while or never stepped onto a platform before, this project will show them how to become a facilitator of learning, not just a presenter. They will build confidence, engage your audience from the beginning and leave your trainees praising your training abilities

This project prepares instructors to present information effectively, respond to participant questions and lead activities that reinforce learning. It encourages the Instructors learn to lead discussions, listen effectively, make accurate observations and help participants to link training to their jobs. It shows how to have the participants to learn to maintain eye contact, maintain a positive attitude, speak in a clear voice, gesture appropriately, and maintain interest and dispel confusion.

1.2 **GOALS OF THE TRAINER**

- To design a module:
- To improve the trainers understanding of the different stages of the training cycle.

- To understand the changing responsibilities of the trainer during different stages of the training cycle.
- To develop a framework for improving the effectiveness of the Training program.

1.3 SCHEMES OF STANDARDS

The expected standards has been presented in six chapters. The scheme of standards is as follows.

Standard 1: Five Hats of a Trainer

- Trainer as a Professional
- Trainer as a Medium
- Trainer as a Facilitator
- Trainer as a Teacher
- Trainer as a Friend & Mentor

Standard 2: Activity suiting Reflector learning styles
Standard 3: Interview of a trainer –

- Training methodology and delivery
- Discipline handling
- Use of learning tools

Standard 4: TNA form

- Fill in the form provided
- Make up the scores as if you have assessed a candidate. Based on the feedback write down the specific feedback you need to provide the candidate that will help him to improve.

Standard 5: Lesson plan on

- Confidence

Standard 6: Voice and Accent

- Phonology
- Blending and Segmentation

- Lessoning
- Elision
- Omission
- Consonant Clusters

•3•

II
FIVE HATS OF A TRAINER

Since trainers are an important part of any company as they are directly responsible for the future growth and performance of their organization.

2.1 TRAINER AS A PROFESSIONAL

In order to wear this hat, a trainer has to understand the following elements that will make them a professional

2.1.2. Professionalism

2.1.3. Importance of professionalism at workplace

2.1.4. Professional vs. nonprofessional

2.1.5. Characteristics of professional

2.1.6. How are you judged as a professional?

2.1.7 Unprofessional behavior

2.1.8 Body Language

2.1.9 Dressing and Personal Grooming

2.1.2. PROFESSIONALISM

- Professionalism in the workplace is based on many factors,

  including how you dress, carry yourself, your attitude and how you interact with others. The definition of professionalism indicates that each person perform their tasks with genuine earnest and honesty. It refers to a person doing his / her job with sincerity, and maintaining

Professional etiquette and ethics in the workplace.
Professionalism is the axis around which any organization
should revolve. A company that chooses not to develop or
enforce policies may end up with a workplace that suffers
from low productivity, low employee morale and poor
customer service.

2.1.3 IMPORTANCE OF PROFESSIONALISM AT WORKPLACE:

- Ensures good performance by all
- Keeps employees motivated
- Ensures a good team spirit
- It is critical to ensure justice and fairness for everyone's efforts
- Helps to maintain the right amount of communication in the workplace

We have seen the importance of Professionalism so far. Now
we will see how trainer can wear the hat of professional.
For that trainer needs to understand what it means to be professional.
And understand the
difference between professional and nonprofessional.

2.1.4. PROFESSIONAL VS NONPROFESSIONAL

- Professional—Knowledge, ideas and information
- Nonprofessional—Work can be measured by the quantity

and quality of work output
Professional

Enter Caption

Enter Caption

Non Professional:

2.1.5. CHARACTERISTICS OF PROFESSIONAL

- Honest
- Skilled
- Courteous
- Reliable
- Considerate
- Dependable
- Cooperative

- Committed

2.1.6. HOW WE ARE JUDGED AS A PROFESSIONAL?

- Your Communication
- Your Image
- Your Competence
- Your Demeanor
- Your Appearance
- Your Behavior
- Your Attitude

2.1.7 UNPROFESSIONAL BEHAVIOR

- Conduct that could be characterized as harassment or discrimination.

- Verbal threats of violence, retribution, or lawsuits.
- Inappropriate physical touching or contact.

Arguing in front of customers, clients and families.

Physical actions that threaten others such as throwing or knocking down objects.

Insults, verbal comments, or criticism intended to belittle Or berate others.

2.1.8 BODY LANGUAGE

Body language is how you carry yourself. So a trainer should always think: Does my body communicate the message I want it to convey?

Positive body language includes:

- Maintaining eye contact with the person to whom you are speaking.
- Smiling (if appropriate) but especially as a greeting and when parting.
- Sitting squarely on a chair, leaning slightly forward (this indicates you are paying attention).
- Nodding in agreement.
- A firm handshake.
- Presenting a calm exterior..

Negative body language includes:

- Not looking at a person when speaking.
- Tapping a foot, fingers etc.
- Rocking backwards and forwards.
- Scratching.
- Continually clearing your throat.
- Fiddling with hair, ear lobes, jewelry, jacket, glasses, etc.
- Picking at fingers or finger nails.
- Yawning.
- Repeatedly looking at your watch or a clock in the room.
- Standing too close to others.
- Inattention to a person who is speaking.

2.1.9. DRESSING & PERSONAL GROOMING:

Dress and language both affect your success and professional image in the workplace. Dressing at or above expectations conveys professionalism and respect for the employer and your colleagues

- An appropriate appearance demonstrates respect for yourself and others.
- Society has established rules regarding appropriate attire and proper presentation for various situations.
- Failure to heed these guidelines is an etiquette gaffe.
- Socially inappropriate attire may cause people to feel uneasy.
- Being well-groomed is more important than being well dressed in the business world.
- People assume that the quality of your work isn't any better than the quality of your appearance.

Best Styles and Colors for Workplace Attire
for Men

Enter Caption

Best Styles and Colors for Workplace Attire
For Women

Enter Caption

While the basic principles of individual professionalism are universal, it is also defined by a set of responsibilities set

forth by an organization for its members to follow.

Incorporating professionalism in the workplace is a critical

element for any company desiring to achieve success. Professionalism is a concerted effort by all within the

workplace to provide the utmost of their ability each and

every day and a concentration on quality of service and

work. It is imperative that management set certain criteria

that all within the organization easily understand and

should follow.

2.2. TRAINER AS A MEDIUM

Trainer should have certain traits to wear this hat. Trainer has to research well on the topic delivered and he/she needs to be well informed as learners perceive them as credible. Trainer needs to take time to get to know their audience to act as better medium. They need to be nonjudgmental, validate everyone's experience and their own right to their own experience and their right to their own perspective. They know that key learning can takes place when people express different viewpoints and bring their own perspectives into adult learning classroom.

2.2.1. A trainer is the medium for transferring knowledge.

- To be medium, trainers needs to possess the subject knowledge.
- This will help the trainer to decide the future training activities. Such a knowledge will help the trainer to select those training methods and materials which suit a particular training course
- Apart from this the trainer needs to possess a broad knowledge of the organization, the general rules, regulations and policies.
- This includes some formal qualification coupled with an understanding of the principles of adult learning and motivation.

2.2.2. A trainer has to possess excellent communication skills to act as a perfect medium.

- Being a good communicator (both is oral and written) is an assets to any trainer. Questioning, explaining, listening, illustrating and preparing training material demand very high communication skills.

2.2.3. To act as a perfect medium, a trainer also needs the following qualities:

- He/She needs to be a role model, be flexible, being value driven being enable, competent, tolerant, patient, developer, learner, innovator a good negotiator, positive thinker, listener, purpose driven, confident, resourceful, empathetic, highly motivated, high performer, disciplined, team builder and visualize.

2.3 TRAINER AS A FACILITATOR

Trainers should understand this role as a facilitator clearly. **A facilitator** is one who has an expert opinion but doesn't offer it unless and until absolutely necessary. The facilitator instead strives to help the participants, usually in a group setting, come to their own conclusions and then summarizes those conclusions for the participants. Where the trainer trains information, the facilitator facilitates the building of consensus.

What is facilitation? Bringing out and focusing the wisdom of the group, often as the group creates something new or solves a problem.

The root of *"facilitate,"* of course, is *"facile,"* or to make a process "easy." The best trainers seem to make learning easy.

Enter Caption

2.3.1 Major Differences between Facilitator and Trainer Roles

Great Facilitator	Great Adult Educator (Trainer)
Is *not* necessarily a content expert.	*Is* a content expert.
Is an expert in many forms of group process (including inter-and-intra-group conflict resolution, strategic planning, team building, etc.)	Is not necessarily expert in many forms of group process. Instead, continually develops new methods to help participants achieve specific learning outcomes.
Often helps the group to define and verbalize its own outcomes (e.g. to solve a specific problem or develop a new procedure.)When outcomes are externally prescribed, helps the group develop, implement and "own" action steps to achieve the outcomes.	Most often in corporate, organizational or higher education settings, the trainer does not help each learner group establish its own learning outcomes. (That's a whole other approach, called Popular Education.) However, the trainer may be involved in implementing and/or analyzing the results of training needs assessments. These should include input from representative (potential) participants as well as other stakeholders.
Sees facilitation as a process to help achieve specific "bits" of broad organizational goals.	Often focuses on training's impact on actual, discrete job performance or tasks. Trainer may evaluate training's effectiveness long after the training event takes place.

Enter Caption

2.3.2 Elements the Two Roles Share

Both great facilitators and the best trainers...

- Help the group achieve specific outcomes through the use ofactive, participatory, participant-centered methods.
- Regularly evaluate the process in real time, and can measure how well the participants achieved the stated outcomes at the end of the process.
- Have made themselves familiar with the organizational culture and context in which they are working, and ensure the processes "fit" that culture.
- Stimulate dialogue and interaction between participants, not just between themselves and the participants.

2.3.3 ATTRIBUTES of an EFFECTIVE FACILITATOR:

- Understand that conflict is a viable part of work place dynamics, whether it is due to differences of opinion, to differences in perception, or even differences in how groups approach the work. Cultural backgrounds often have an impact on these dynamics as well.

- Remain neutral so you can help both parties engage with each other in conversation.
- Be knowledgeable about your belief systems and not allow these systems to interfere with the process if the group is going somewhere that would conflict with your beliefs. Know when to remove yourself, if necessary.
- Be aware of your own hot buttons that would make it hard to remain objective.
- Understand how groups function and do homework on group norms.
- Be knowledgeable about different cultures within the organization or educational institution and in the room (e.g. engineers, marketing people, Latinos, Asians, international individuals/groups, etc.).
- Be able to refer participants to resources that go beyond the scope of the particular class or group session.

- **2.3.4 SKILLS of an EFFECTIVE FACILITATOR:**

1. The ability to be "process oriented" or be able to focus on the "how"
2. Ability to help participants overcome their resistance to change
3. Listening, not only to what is said, but for what is NOT said
4. Ability to describe the dynamics going on in the room (i.e. to describe specific behaviors of others, and then build bridges where you see gaps in the communication process)
5. Ability to give constructive feedback and coach individuals
6. Ability to describe your own discomfort with a process
7. Ability to endure a certain amount of discomfort. There will come a time in the facilitation process when the group will appear to be floundering. As a facilitator, you must learn when to allow for silence, and when to intervene. You need to be in touch with your own level of discomfort and tolerance for such ambiguity.
8. Faith in the process. This is when the magic of facilitation comes alive.

2.4 TRAINERS AS A TEACHER

A Trainer should understand the difference between the teaching and training in order to be an effective trainer.

First, let's look at definitions for these activities in the *Merriam-Webster Online Dictionary*.

"Teach" have many alternate definitions, including:

- To cause to know something
- To guide the studies of
- To impart the knowledge of
- To instruct by precept, example, or experience

Definitions for *train* are:

To form by instruction, discipline, or drill

To make prepared for a test of skill

A trainer should understand the there is lot of difference between Teaching and Training.

A trainer should understand that there is a significant difference between teaching and training.

For example, teaching often focuses on theoretical knowledge and conceptual understanding. In a classroom setting, a teacher might lecture on the principles of economics, explaining various theories and models to help students understand how economies function. The primary goal is to impart knowledge and ensure that students can recall and discuss these concepts.

In contrast, training is more practical and skills-oriented. For instance, in a corporate environment, a trainer might conduct a workshop on effective sales techniques. This would involve role-playing exercises, real-life scenario simulations, and hands-on practice. The aim is to equip participants with specific skills they can immediately apply in their job, such as how to close a sale or handle customer objections effectively.

In summary, while teaching is about knowledge transfer and intellectual development, training is about skill development and practical application.

Teaching	Training
Teaching provides new knowledge to the people.	Training helps the already knowledgeable people to learn the tools and techniques to apply the same.
Teaching on education, knowledge and wisdom with a longer time span.	Training lays stress on skills and abilities with a shorter time span
Teaching gives extensive domains with limited knowledge in general.	Training gives intensive information about a limited domain.
Teaching provides breadth of knowledge in all spheres.	In other words, training provides depth of knowledge in a specific sphere.
Teaching is, in general, a broader area.	Training is for a specific area
· Teacher provides information, knowledge, and experience.	Trainer facilitates learning.
Teacher usually creates the 'need to know' the knowledge for students	In training, the student himself approaches for the knowledge as he realizes the need to know.
Generally teacher provides feedback to students.	On the other hand, the trainer gets feedback from trainees.

Enter Caption

2.4.1Difference between Teaching and Training.

Hence a trainer may need to wear the teacher hat when their trainees don't have subject knowledge. After causing them to know the subject knowledge then he/ she need to switch to trainer's role to get the students to practice the knowledge through practices.

2.5 TRAINER AS A FRIEND & MENTOR

Many trainers wonder what are the differences between a trainer, mentor, indeed, this can be very confusing because both the trainer and mentor often will do more than what they are responsible for, perhaps because they are helpful by nature. Otherwise, they will not be doing what they are doing in the first place.

It will be good if we could look at how Oxford Dictionary defines them:

- **Trainer:** a person who trains people or animals.

- **Mentor:** an experienced and trusted adviser.

As for the mentor, it should be clear by now that he does not impart any technical knowledge or skills, nor is he involved in any implementation work; he is usually a general adviser without any involvement in the mentee's work.

Responsibilities	Trainer	Mentor
Imparts technical knowledge and skills	Yes.	Generally no, or probably just some random sharing.
Offers advice on...	No, there is no expectation to do so.	Beliefs, values, mindset and personal development
Comes up with solutions, and / or be directly involved in implementation	No, there is no expectation to do so.	No, the focus is not on problem-solving.
Duration	Course period (short-term)	On-going (long-term)

Enter Caption

2.5.1Mentoring: is a deliberate pairing of a highly skilled individual with a less experienced person for the purpose of helping the less skilled person develops specific competencies. It differs from coaching. You can coach many people with varying levels of experience at the same time. Mentoring is a focused relationship with one person or a few individuals.

Mentoring is not for everyone. A mentor and mentee have to have specific qualities. The relationship has to have specific goals. A discussion of these qualities and goals will help trainers determine if they should become involved in a mentoring relationship.

2.5.2Mentors should have several key skills including:

1. **Strong Interpersonal Skills:** Mentors must effectively talk and listen, demonstrating empathy and understanding. They believe in the potential for improvement in others.

2. **Professional Involvement:** This includes having a robust network of peers and resources that can assist the mentee, leveraging these

connections for the mentee's benefit.

3. **Excellent Supervisory Skills:** Effective mentors are proficient at managing and guiding people, ensuring that they can provide constructive feedback and support.

4. **Technical Competence:** Mentors should have a thorough knowledge of their field, ensuring they can provide accurate and relevant guidance.

5. **Personal Power:** Mentors have high self-esteem and command respect, with others often seeking their opinions and advice.

6. **Motivation:** A mentor should maintain their own interest and enthusiasm in their profession, which is often enhanced through the mentoring relationship with their mentee. This ongoing motivation contributes to their effectiveness as a mentor.

7. **Empathy:**

ax. Demonstrating genuine concern for the mentee's well-being.
ax. Recognizing and validating the mentee's emotions and experiences.
ax. Offering support in both professional and personal challenges.

8. **Patience:**

ax. Understanding that learning and growth take time.
ax. Remaining calm and composed when mentees make mistakes.
ax. Encouraging persistence and resilience in mentees.

9. **Adaptability:**

ax. Tailoring mentoring techniques to suit different learning styles and personalities.
ax. Being open to change and new approaches.
ax. Adjusting goals and plans based on the mentee's progress and feedback.

10. **Active Listening:**

ax. Avoiding interruptions and giving the mentee full attention.
ax. Asking clarifying questions to ensure understanding.
ax. Reflecting on and summarizing what the mentee has shared.

11. **Conflict Resolution:**

ax. Identifying potential sources of conflict early on.
ax. Facilitating open and honest communication between parties.
ax. Developing strategies for mutually beneficial solutions.

12. **Goal-Oriented:**

ax. Helping mentees break down large goals into manageable steps.
ax. Setting SMART (Specific, Measurable, Achievable, Relevant, Time-bound) goals.
ax. Monitoring and adjusting goals as needed based on progress.

13. **Confidentiality:**

ax. Establishing clear boundaries and expectations regarding privacy.
ax. Ensuring sensitive information is protected.
ax. Building trust through consistent and reliable confidentiality practices.

14. **Inspirational:**

ax. Sharing personal success stories and experiences.
ax. Encouraging a positive mindset and can-do attitude.
ax. Celebrating the mentee's achievements and milestones.

15. **Constructive Feedback:**

ax. Providing feedback in a timely manner.
ax. Balancing positive reinforcement with areas for improvement.
ax. Using specific examples to illustrate points.

16. **Lifelong Learning:**

ax. Staying updated with industry trends and best practices.
ax. Seeking out new learning opportunities and experiences.
ax. Demonstrating a commitment to continuous self-improvement.

17. **Cultural Competence:**

ax. Being aware of and respectful towards diverse backgrounds.

ax.   Incorporating cultural awareness into mentoring practices.
ax.   Addressing any biases or prejudices constructively.

18.   **Problem-Solving Skills:**

ax.   Encouraging mentees to analyze and understand problems thoroughly.
ax.   Guiding mentees through brainstorming potential solutions.
ax.   Helping mentees develop critical thinking and decision-making skills.

19.   **Encouragement of Independence:**

ax.   Promoting self-reliance and accountability.
ax.   Providing opportunities for mentees to lead and make decisions.
ax.   Supporting mentees in taking risks and learning from outcomes.

20.   **Time Management:**

ax.   Teaching mentees prioritization and time-blocking techniques.
ax.   Helping mentees set realistic timelines and deadlines.
ax.   Providing tools and resources to manage time effectively.

21.   **Networking:**

ax.   Introducing mentees to key industry contacts.
ax.   Encouraging participation in professional events and organizations.
ax.   Teaching effective networking and relationship-building strategies.

22.   **Emotional Intelligence:**

ax.   Practicing self-awareness and self-regulation.
ax.   Recognizing and managing emotions in oneself and others.
ax.   Using emotional insights to enhance communication and relationships.

Mentors possess a diverse range of key skills essential for guiding and nurturing their mentees' growth. These include strong interpersonal communication, professional involvement, and technical competence. Additionally, mentors exhibit empathy, patience, and adaptability, fostering a supportive environment for mentees to thrive. They actively listen, resolve conflicts, and set SMART goals, all while maintaining confidentiality and inspiring confidence. Emphasizing lifelong learning and cultural competence, mentors encourage independence, provide constructive feedback, and adeptly manage time. Furthermore, they facilitate networking opportunities and demonstrate emotional intelligence in guiding mentees towards success.

2.5.3 A mentee, or the protégé of the mentor, should

- Take on the responsibility for their own development-mentors should help and not take responsibility for this process.
- Desire to achieve results-mentoring is goal directed and not just to make you feel good.
- Value feedback even if it is not positive

2.5.4 Objectives for Mentoring

- Provide an atmosphere of friendship and learning
- Provide instruction on specified skill
- Provide challenges, assignments, critiques, encouragement and support
- To allow time and space for growth, not time constraints
- To assist in developing projects, assignments and course materials using technology
- To explore basics about computer uses and applications
- To discuss the fundamentals about online active curriculum

2.5.5 Mentoring:

- Set up a meeting schedule that works best for both mentor and mentee. It's a good idea to avoid, lunch and coffee break meeting. Meetings require a professional and distraction-free setting.
- Maintaining regular meetings between mentor and mentee is the best way to keep both parties engaged. Even if there are no urgent items of the agenda, avoid cancelling or putting off the meeting to a later date.
- Setup regular meeting dates in advance so both parties have time to fully prepare.
- Aim for quality of meetings, not quantity. Find ways to use your time as efficiently as possible so you can cover the most ground (but don't rush!).

- Both the mentor and mentee should make themselves available in between face-to-face meetings for phone and/or email contact when required.
- Show interest and commitment to the relationship (through actions before words) by arriving at meetings on time and prepared, responding promptly to emails and phone messages and sharing openly and respectfully.
- Recognize that building trust requires time and effort from both parties.
- Alternate meeting locations between each other's worksites.
- Stay curious and do not be afraid to ask each other questions at meetings.
- Remember that mentoring is a two-way street – be sure that you are both using these meetings as an opportunity to learn!

2.5.6 Mentoring Relationship:

A mentoring relationship is a professional or personal partnership in which an experienced individual, known as a mentor, provides guidance, support, and advice to a less experienced person, called a mentee. The main goal of this relationship is to foster the mentee's development, both professionally and personally, by leveraging the mentor's knowledge, experience, and insights.

Types of Mentoring:

Formal Mentoring: Structured programs often facilitated by organizations, with defined goals, processes, and timeframes.

Informal Mentoring: More casual and spontaneous, often developing naturally out of professional or personal relationships.

Peer Mentoring: Involves individuals at similar levels of experience and status providing mutual support.

Group Mentoring: One mentor works with multiple mentees simultaneously, or several mentors collaborate to support a group of mentees.

Overall, mentoring relationships are dynamic and adaptable, capable of evolving to meet the changing needs and goals of both the mentor and the mentee.

2.5.7 Roles in Mentoring

A **mentor** should provide gateways to important areas, and should take on many roles as follows.

- **A guide;** planning, leading, directing, correcting, they should be positive, the mentor should provide motivation and encouragement, guide the learner in his process of learning, and provide a map of the learning; a plan of direction, as well as the reason for the direction. The mentor should guide the learner in determining what he needs to learn, and together they should structure the map.
- **A resource;** allowing their learner to ask questions without fear of ridicule, disappointment or belittlement. The mentor should be the resource to the learner concerning anything about their topic.
- **A support;** communication, open availability, encouragement, humor, trust, care, positive affirmation, gentle critiquing. Supports the learner in rethinking his learning, in order to gain the knowledge he seeks.
- **A connection;** giving the student the ability to resource for the learner, to intervene in the learner's learning experience, providing a connection to the learning in new, concise ways. Involving, impressing on the learner the importance of taking his learning into his own hands, to be responsible to learn, while mentoring and later on his own. Helping him to gain the love of learning for a lifetime. The learner needs to feel connected with the learning. The mentor needs to be connected with the learner, his strengths, weaknesses, and stress level and level of excitement.
- **An active participant. In** order for the learning to be lasting, the learner must be allowed, and even expected to do the work of his learning instruction completely on his own. The mentor has the role of a participant in the learning with the learner, but the learner should be the one who is moving his own learning, not the mentor. There should also be an active dialog between the mentor and the learner. The communication between the two participants must continually be two-way, allowing complete communication of ideas, issues and collaboration. The mentor should always see the learner as another way that he (himself) might learn to teach and mentor more effectively.

2.5.8 Expectations for Mentoring
Learner Expectations

- To be learn computer applications

- To become more equipped for technological application
- To learn how to integrate technology with classroom instruction
- To be challenged in the learning of technology

- To be treated respectfully
- To get frustrated and learn how to work through the frustrations

Mentor Expectations

- To work closely
- To be available often, on an "on call" basis
- To assist in the learning of the participant
- To challenge the learner
- To be challenged by the learner

III

ACTIVITIES SUITING THE LEARNING STYLES

The purpose of this chapter is to provide with an understanding of the importance of learning, and how understanding the preferences for learning can assist in maximizing the benefit the trainers can gain from the whole range of learning experiences they are bound to encounter during their lifetime.

3.1 Understanding the preferred learning styles

As a trainer, it is useful to understand the preferred learning styles of each team member so that they can support them to develop their performance. This understanding will assist trainers in discussing the professional development and support options that will best suit a team member's needs and how they prefer to learn.

These learning styles are only a guide. A team member will have a mixture of these styles and their preferred style will change depending on the type of activity being undertaken. The labels are not as important as being able to recognise the characteristics of each style and modify professional development and support options accordingly.

A brief outline of each style is given overleaf, including how team members with this preferred style learn best and how learning can be hindered. Learning Style Descriptors (Honey and Munford, 1999)

Reflector – Reviewers	Activist – Doers
Reflectors prefer to view things from different perspectives with an opportunity to plan ahead, attend to detail and look for the meaning of things.	Activists enjoy new and challenging activities, and benefit most from learning through experience and working with others.
Theorist – Conclude	**Pragmatist – Planners**
Theorists benefit most from learning through models, theories or concepts, and analyzing ideas logically within structured environments.	Pragmatists learn most easily through immediate practical application of activities with an obvious link between subject matter and "real life" applications.

Enter Caption

The four Learning Styles are linked with the steps we go through as we learn.

Reference

Swailes, S. and Senior, B. (2002) The Dimensionality of Honey and Mumford's Learning Styles Questionnaire International Journal of Selection and Assessment .Volume 7, Issue 1, pages 1–11, March 1999

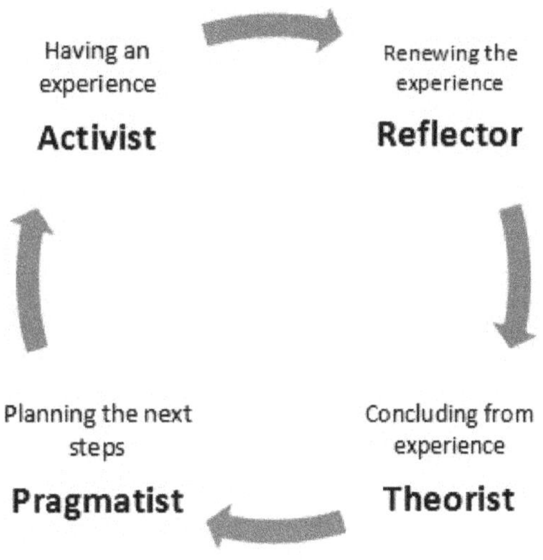

Enter Caption

Activist

Activists are those people who learn by doing. Activists need to get their hands dirty, to dive in with both feet first. Have an open-minded approach to learning, involving themselves fully and without bias in new experiences

Activities that suits them

- brainstorming
- problem solving
- group discussion
- puzzles
- competitions
- role-play

Theorist

These learners like to understand the theory behind the actions. They need models, concepts and facts in order to engage in the learning process. Prefer to analyze and synthesize, drawing new information into a systematic and logical 'theory'.

Activities that suits them

- models
- statistics
- stories
- quotes
- background information
- applying theories

Pragmatist

These people need to be able to see how to put the learning into practice in the real world. Abstract concepts and games are of limited use unless they can see a way to put the ideas into action in their lives. Experimenters, trying out new ideas, theories and techniques to see if they work.

Activities that suits them

- time to think about how to
- apply learning in reality
- case studies
- problem solving

- discussion

Reflector

These people learn by observing and thinking about what happened. They may avoid leaping in and prefer to watch from the sidelines. Prefer to stand back and view experiences from a number of different perspectives, collecting data and taking the time to work towards an appropriate conclusion.

Activities that suits them

- paired discussions
- self analysis questionnaires
- personality questionnaires
- time out
- observing activities
- feedback from others
- coaching
- interviews

- As we have seen the activities that suits all different learning styles, now let us look into couple of example where activities are presented as follows.

1. Activity that suits for reflectors
2. Activity that suits all learning styles type.

3.2 Learning activity that suits Reflectors:

Role-play

Name: ____

Question Bank

1. Tell me about yourself
2. What would you describe as your weakness/strength?
3. Why do you want to work for us?
4. What has been your biggest professional achievement?
5. Why did you leave your last job?
6. What salary range are you looking?
7. What do you know about our company?

8.   What did you like about your previous job?
9.   How do you handle stress and pressure?
10.   Why should we hire you?

JUDGING ITEMS	EXCELLENT	GOOD	FAIR
Speech Development Logic, Ideas, Thought flow			
Correctness Pronunciation, Word selection			
Delivery Confident, eye contact/gestures, clear voice			

Enter Caption

3.3 Learning activity that suits all the 4 learning styles.

- **Read the answering machine message**
- **Complete the questions with the following questions words:**

  - **What(4)- Where(2) - which – How much – Who(2)**

- **Find and write answers to your questions in the "Your answer" Column**

  After completing, Do the following activity with a partner.

- **Listen to your partners message and complete the "B answers column"**
- **If necessary ask the question to complete the "B answer column"**

Hey there John, It's Kevin. How's it going? I want to know if you want to see a film with me this evening. There two films at Capital Cinema in Oxford and it's not an expensive theatre, only 6.25$ for a ticket. The first one is "Happiness Therapy". It is a romantic comedy and it is playing at 5.45 this evening. The second one is a horror film called "Haunted" and it starts at 7.10PM. I prefer going to see something funny but you can choose. Give me a call at home, my number is

061649866. Hope to hear from you, Bye!.

Questions	Your answer	B's answer
______________ is calling?		
______________ is the message for?		
______________ is the name of the theatre?		
______________ is the theatre located(City)		
______________ does a ticket cost?		
______________ are the names of the films?		
______________ Time are the film playing?		
______________ does the caller prefer to see?		
______________ is the caller calling from?		
______________ is the caller's phone no?		

Enter Caption

IV

INTERVIEW OF A TRAINER

I have interviewed the trainer named Mrs. Bharthi who works as a freelancer at an Institute which deals with training students on communication skills and make them employable at various industries. As I have completed the interview these are my findings on Training Methodologies, Deliveries & Learning tools.

The structure of the training is as follows.

<table>
<tr><td colspan="4">TRAINING METHODOLOGIES AND DELIVERY</td></tr>
<tr><td>Instructor led Training</td><td>Computer Based Training</td><td>Practice</td><td>Evaluation</td></tr>
<tr><td></td><td></td><td></td><td></td></tr>
</table>

<table>
<tr><td colspan="8">LEARNING TOOLS</td></tr>
<tr><td>Stories</td><td>Lesson</td><td>Simulation</td><td>Hands on activity</td><td>Field Visit</td><td>Free Speech</td><td>Group Discussion</td><td>Role play & Games</td></tr>
</table>

Enter Caption

4.1 TRAINING METHODOLOGIES AND DELIVERY

In this organization, she plans her training methodologies in four levels that will lead the participants towards the training purpose.

4.1.1 INSTRUCTOR LEAD TRAINING

Here she prepares their participants to build work skills, soft skills and personality development. The program is bilingual & interactive which helps overcome the students MTI (Mother Tongue Influence) problem, English speaking, grammar, public speaking and host of other challenges that participants face in their endeavor to become world class professionals.

4.1.2 COMPUTER BASED TRAINING:

She focuses on audio-visual and learning with hands-on training.

- **She equips students with an in depth subject knowledge on soft skills and inducts the student with 60% student centric activities.**

4.1.3 PRACTICE:

- Interactive digitized solution ensures holistic development of participants and maximizes their engagement and participation.

- Developed under an interactive and stimulating environment, the student centric digitized content instills cognitive thinking among the learners through quizzes, simulations, games, videos and assessments embedded in it.

4.1.4 EVALUATION:

- Finally all the participants will be evaluated by undergoing through various activities.

- Video based scenarios, role plays, activities and interaction, this helps in providing real time experience

- Through this real time experience, she builds confidence in the students and make them professionals in their job roles.

4.2 LEARNING TOOLS

Following learning tools are used by her to train the participants. She uses these learning tools by which they make learning fun, faster and easier.

4.2.1stories:

- Sharing Success and inspiring stories make the participants feel fresh, calm and relaxed before starting daily session.

4.2.2 Lesson:

- Here she trains the participants on soft skills, using a blend of teaching, training and facilitation methods to keep it participants oriented.

- Here she ensures to employ different activities to meet the needs of various learning styles.

4.2.3SIMULATION:

- Computer based techniques (digitization) ensures better understanding of theoretical as well as practical sessions.

4.2.4hands on activity:

- She engages the participants with hands-on training as she believes that until participants practice on their own, they would not be able to understand completely.

4.2.5FIELD VISIT:

- As a trainer, she encourages the participants to visit different professionals which will help them to understand the real life exposure of the training that they provide. This helps their participants to be in sync with the dynamic professional world.

4.2.6free speech:

- She establishes an open minded culture where participants can share their ideas or views freely without worrying about making mistakes. This allows her participants to have fair chances to express themselves and build confidence in them.

4.2.7group discussion:

- She asks questions through quizzes and other intellectual activities that which helps her to monitor the level of understanding.

4.2.8 Role play & GAMES:

- To keep participant's interest level intact, she conducts various activities during session. These activities include mind-map, triad review, shuffle, etc.

- She strongly believes in developing a sense of social and job etiquette that will help the participants become presentable and confident to perform well in the industry.

1. **DISCIPLINE HANDLING**

This organization follows a progressive discipline plan. In progressive discipline, each step is followed by another, providing students with several opportunities to modify their behavior.

For typical classroom situations, the following list of 10 progressive discipline steps are implemented.

Step 1: Redirect Student Behavior

Redirect student behavior by verbally or non-verbally pointing out to the student what he or she should be doing. Standing near a student who is off-task or asking a student a clarifying question can serve as effective types of redirection.

Step 2: Face-to-Face Conference with the Student

Most of the trainers have found that the best way to carry out this step is to schedule a quick meeting after class with the student, before he or she goes to the next class. Just pull a student aside and communicate your behavior expectations and provide the student with an opportunity to respond.

Step 3: Change the student's seating assignment.

This often works quite well, particularly if neighboring students seem to be encouraging the misbehavior.

The front row, closest to the teacher, is a good spot for relocation, although we can use the seats in the back row for attention-seeking students on occasion.

Step 4: Informally discuss options with your fellow teaching teammates and/or support staff.

Use this opportunity to express your concerns and look for any input or behavior strategies that may be working in their other classes.

Step 5: Time out.

Relocate the student to another teacher's classroom for a time out. If the previous four steps have been implemented and the behavior continues, you can send that student to a pre-arranged time-out room.

It's a good practice to notify the partnering teacher that you are sending the student. After all, we are placing a misbehaving student in his or her class. With that in mind, always provide work for the student to complete while in the other teacher's class.

Step 6: Contact the parent, preferably by phone.

Always begin your call on a positive note by noting ways that the student is being successful. After that, communicate your concerns along with the process that you have already taken to correct the situation.

Make sure to take notes, provide contact information, and to express your eagerness to partner with the parent throughout the process.

Step 7: If the behavior persists, assign a detention.

Detentions can be served before or after school, or if the administration allows, during lunch.

Detention can be effective, particularly if the student must complete a task that he or she would not normally undertake. Of course, it DOES require you to put in extra time as well.

Step 8: Write a guidance referral.

Depending on your situation, you may be able to send the offending student directly to the guidance office at the time of the infraction. If not, you may be able to schedule a conference with the counselor.

If possible, provide your written documentation of the behavior interventions that you have taken for the guidance counselor's reference.

Step 9: Meet with your direct supervisor

Provide them with the documentation you have collected during behavior intervention. Seek their counsel and direction.

Step 10: Write a detailed discipline referral to your administrator.

Trust that the administrator will make the right decision for the student based on the documentation.

V
TRAINING NEED ANALYISIS

OBJECTIVE:

To achieve successful results in training, a trainer needs to evaluate the assimilation levels of the participants. This module will deal setting assessment parameters and levels, designing a scoring pattern based on the parameters and understanding what the achievable results would be at the end of the training program.

Most importantly, we will learn how to use effective feedback techniques when communicating the results of these assessments.

Topics:

- Training Needs Analysis
- Giving Feedback
- Taking Feedback
- Feedback Techniques

Parameters	5	4	3	2	1	Comments
A. Voice Quality						
1. Articulation of sounds						
Consonant sounds						
Vowel Sounds						
2. Pronounciation of words						
Correct Syllable Stress						
No mispronunciation						
3. Inflection						
Emphasizes words to enhance meaning						
Is congruent with the meaning of the words						
4. Voice Modulation						
No monotone						
Expresses appropriate Emotion or Feeling						
5. Intensity / Pitch						
How high or deep the voice sounds						
Conveys the appropriate understanding						
6. Rate of Speech						
Clear and understandable						
Matched to the pace of other person						
Total Score						
Total Level						

Enter Caption

5.2 FEEDBACK:

1. ### **Articulation of sounds**

- Keep all vowels, sounds, open, full and rounded.
- Articulate sounds, vowels and consonants clearly and distinctly with your tongue, teeth and palate.
- Pronounce every syllable in every word.

2. Pronunciation of words

- Try find a conversation partner. Let your partner know about the areas of pronunciation you would like to work on, and ask him to give you feedback and corrections for improvement. You may want to practice reading a story or article aloud with a learning partner to check your pronunciation.

- Practice in front of a mirror, so that you can see your lips and tongue moving into position to create each sound. Seeing yourself pronounce each sound can reinforce what you have learned about how the sounds are made.

3. Inflection

- You end sentences with upward inflections, you sound like you are asking questions, and it makes you sound uncertain. Try and have your statements firm with downward inflection. You will sound great.

4. Voice Modulation

- Try to lower your voice and slow down if you are speaking too quickly. Pause momentarily in between sentences to control your pace better. In that way you will sound much better. Otherwise you are doing great.

5. Intensity / Pitch

- You are sounding too high when you speak due to nerves or stress. It makes you sound less confident. If you slow down, breathe, and try to speak in your normal pitch, you will sound confident.

6. Rate of Speech

- Refrain from running your words together. You finish each word by articulating clearly the final letter.

- Open your mouth wider, enunciate more clearly, and pause more frequently. These will help you sound less rushed.

- Slow down for important points. By slowing your speech rate while delivering your key points, you can convey emphasis and importance.

Speed up when you want to share your excitement, or when telling a story for illustration.

VI

LESSON PLAN ON CONFIDENCE

Confidence

Objectives: To increase participants' confidence level

Goals: To help them to see for themselves how confiden

Activity Details			
Presentation(Trainer Activity)	Practice –(Student Activity)	Production	Resources
Divide group into pairs and ask each participant to cite a situation where they felt lacking in confidence. Divide group into pairs again, repeat process but citing examples of confidence. Labels Exercise – Split group into 2 groups. Ask I group to write down all the negative words that have been used to describe women/men. Ask the other group to write down all the positive words that have been used to describe them.(this will be more difficult)	In groups, one person takes several minutes to describe their experience etc while the other listens. As above but citing experiences of feeling confident. Students split into 2 groups		Flip Chart paper Pens
Group with magazines and ask them to cut out pictures which portray confidence. Stick pictures on to flip chart sheets explaining reasons for choices.	explanation for choice		Pens Scissors Flip chart paper
Tutor describes an imaginary line in the room that has a scale attached to it, with not all confident at one end of the line to very confident at the other end of the line.	Students to physically position themselves on line.	Describe each situation in turn (see handout A) and ask each participant to physically place herself on the imaginary line according to how confident she generally feels in each situation.	Handout
They then pass their paper to their neighbor on the left who has to fill in a balloon writing in something positive about the named person. Everyone then passes the paper on to the person on the left and so on until your paper comes back to you. After giving everyone an opportunity to read through their own paper, ask each participant to read to the group 2 of the things written about them.	Each participant is given an opportunity to read through their own paper, asking them to read to the rest of the group 2 of the things written about them.	Discuss with them how are they feeling. Appreciate and leave them with a positive note that they can do great.	Markers Paper Balloons

Enter Caption

Post Training Reflection:
Follow up with the students and ensure that they come up with an action
plan to build confidence.

VII
VOICE AND ACCENT

7.1 PHONOLOGY:
PHONETICS/PHONOLOGY:

The **branch of linguistics** which studies the use of sound in human language. Phonetics is the study of the physical nature of speech sounds and speech production: how sounds are produced by the human body, what they are like as sound waves, and how the human ear processes speech.

Phonology is the study of how sound is structured in languages -- for instance, which of all possible speech sounds a language uses to build its words, how syllables are built in a particular language, and other phenomena.

In order for a group of sounds to be a natural class, it must include *all* of the sounds that share a particular feature or group of features, and not include sounds that *don't.*

7.1.1 Based on *articulation* or *production*:

For example, both *labio-dental* and *bilabial* involve the lips.

Therefore, we can group them together under the term *labial.*

In English, these sounds are [m, b, p, f, v, w]

In English, the sound [w] doesn't occur after any of these sounds. We can use the term *labial* to simplify the description: [w] doesn't occur after **labial sounds**.

7.1.2 Based on sound quality, or *auditory* properties.

One example of a natural class based on auditory properties is *Sibilants.* Take a look at the pronunciation of the plural suffix in English, which we will label *-s*

This suffix is pronounced in three different ways, depending on the last sound in the noun to which it is added.

If the noun ends with a *voiced* sound the phonetic form is [z].If the noun ends in a *voiceless* sound the phonetic form is [s].

However, after such words as *rich, bush, kiss, garages, rouge,* and *maze,* (in other words, [s, z, S, Z, tS, dZ,]) the form is [«z].

This group of sounds all differs in respect to voicing, place, and manner of articulation. However, they do have an auditory property in common: a *high pitched hissing sound.*

These sounds, therefore, form a natural class called *sibilants.* So using this natural class, we can state a generalization:

+ plural à [«z] / after a *sibilant*

This rule states that the sound occurs in a general context, rather than having to specify for each individual context.

7.1.3 Other classes include:

Obstruents, which are sounds produced with an 'obstruction' of air flow, namely stops, fricatives, affricates.

Sonorants, which are consonants produced with a relatively open passage for the air flow, including nasals, approximants and others (or nasals, liquids, glides, and others).

7.1.4 Phonetic Rules:

A speaker's knowledge of phonological rules allows him or her to "translate" phonemes into actual sounds. Knowledge of these rules forms part of a speaker's *linguistic competence.*

The following is a representation of the process:

Phonemic form

ä

rules

ä

phonetic form

In other words, phonological rules apply to the phonemic form to produce the phonetic form.

To accept this is to accept the notion that there is something called an **underlying form.** In the linguistic literature, this underlying form is called the **Underlying Representation** or **UR.**

There are several different ways that we can classify phonological rules.

7.1.4a Assimilation.

- Rules involving assimilation cause a sound to become more like a neighboring sound with respect to some feature.
- In other words, the segment affected by the rule *assimilates* or *takes on a feature from a nearby (usually adjacent) sound.*

- For example:.

I can ask [ay kæn æsk]
I can bake [ay kæm bek]
I can go [ay kæŋ go]

- Another example is *vowel nasalization:*

pit [pHIt] pin [pHIân]

7.1.4b Dissimilation. Rules involving dissimilation cause two neighboring sounds to become *less alike with respect to some feature.*

- Dissimilation rules are less common than assimilation rules, at least in English.

One example of a dissimilation rule is *fricative dissimilation:*
/θ/ changes to [t] following another fricative:
fifth phonemically [fIfθ]
phonetically often realized as [fIft]
sixth phonemically [sIksθ]
but often realized as [sIkst]
Another classification is **insertion** (also called **epenthesis**).

7.1.4c Rules of insertion *cause a segment not present at the phonemic level to be added to the phonetic realization of a word.*

One example of an insertion rule is *voiceless stop insertion.* Between a nasal and a voiceless fricative, a voiceless stop with the same place of articulation as the nasal is inserted.

strength /strɛŋθ/ → [strɛŋkθ]
hampster /hæmster/ → [hæmpster]

7.1.4d Deletion. Deletion rules eliminate a sound. Such rules apply more frequently to unstressed syllables and in casual speech.

/h/ - deletion: /h/ may be deleted in unstressed syllables.

In the sentence, 'He handed her his hat,' the **UR** is:

/hi hænd«d h«r hIz hQt/

but is often represented on the surface as:

[hi hænd«d «r Iz hQt]

7.1.4e Metathesis

These rules change the order of sounds

The Format for representing Phonological Rules

The basic format for specifying phonological rules is as follows:

A → B/ C __ D

This format is meant to be read as "A becomes B in the environment following C and preceding D."

For example, here are the formulations for two of the rules we have discussed so far:

Vowel → + nasal/ ___ nasal

Alveolar → + dental/ ____ dental

7.2 BLENDING AND SEGMENTATION

Segmenting

- Segmenting means breaking the words up into their component sounds. For

  example, the word 'blue' has three sounds /b/, /l/ and /u:/. The two letters **ue** are
  one sound. The word cat also has three sounds /k/ /æ/ and /t/. The word shop also
  has three sounds /ʃ/, /ɒ/ and /p/. The letters **sh** are one sound.

- Students need to learn to look at a word and immediately know exactly how many

  sounds there are in that word and what those sounds are (segmenting).

- Students can do this only when they know the sounds well.

- Students must be guided by the trainer and the trainer must know which sounds

  the students know and which they do not know. For example, the word blue contains the sound /u:/ which is not taught to year 1 students. Therefore, year 1

students cannot segment the word blue and so in year 1 blue is a sight word.

- In the beginning the trainer guides the students by helping them to segment. The

trainer might start out by segmenting words for the students, while doing the action

for each sound. The trainer might progress to saying the word very slowly and

exaggerating or elongating the sounds while doing the actions. The trainer may

then say the word normally but tell students how many sounds there are in the

word.

- Ultimately, through whatever means necessary, the students should be able to hear

a word spoken normally and know exactly how many sounds in the word and what

those sounds are.

Blending

- Blending is when students combine (blend) sounds together in a logical way to read a word.

- Students must be taught exactly how to blend sounds, that is, they must be taught steps.

- Students must learn that when blending sounds it is necessary to group certain

- Sounds together is stages so that the blended sounds begin to sound like the word.

- Therefore, students must learn which sounds go together

- For example, the word cat can be read two ways

1. c + a = ca. 2. a + t = at
ca + t = cat c + at = cat

7.3 LIASONING

- Liaison is the pronunciation of a final and normally silent consonant in a word when that word precedes certain other words. Liaison is a prominent feature of French but is not otherwise very common among languages.
- It is the pronunciation of an otherwise absent consonant sound at the end of the first of two consecutive words the second of which begins with a vowel sound and follows without pause.
- Non-native speakers need to perfect the vowels and consonants of Standard American English to sound less accented. However, another important aspect of accent reduction is using the appropriate rhythm and intonation. An important way to facilitate a smoother liason between words is to use contractions in everyday conversation.

Contractions Facilitate Smoothness

- Americans do not use contractions when they are writing formally, however, when writing casually and when speaking conversationally, we always shorten our sentences with the use of contractions. The use of contractions facilitates a smoother link between words and allows us to sound more casual. When we do not use contractions, we sound more formal and the smooth flow of speech is interrupted.

What Is A Contraction?

- A contraction is formed by combining two words into one and by using an apostrophe to substitute for the letter or letters that have been omitted. The following is a list of the more frequently used contractions:

  - I'll I will
  - I'm I am

- Can't Can not
- Won't Will not
- Isn't Is not
- She'll She will
- He'll He will
- He's He is
- Wasn't Was not
- Weren't Were not
- Shouldn't Should not
- Wouldn't Would not

7.4 ELISION

Elision is the omission of sounds, syllables or words in speech. This is done to make the language easier to say, and faster.

- Example
'I don't know' /I duno/ , /kamra/ for camera, and 'fish 'n' chips' are all examples of elision.

Elision is an important area in listening skills, as learners are often unable to hear elided words correctly, especially if they have little contact with native speakers. Word-counting and dictations are two activities that practice recognition, whilst at the production stage drilling elided forms such as contracted forms is common.

Elision is all about dropping sounds or not pronouncing them fully in fluent

speech.

- In English, stress placement in sentences and rhythm are part and parcel of everyday

speech. As a result, stress placement is variable depending upon the meaning and the effect sought. This is quite a large area of phonetics, so for now we will simply identify

some regular features of stress placement in connected utterances. Some words regularly

attract the stress, while others don't. Those that are regularly unstressed are:

- **auxiliary verbs – primary and modal**
- **determiners (articles, demonstrative pronouns, etc.)**
- **subject pronouns (he, she, it, they, etc.)**
- **prepositions (one/two syllable words e.g. on, in, at, upon, etc.)**
- **conjunctions (and, but, so, etc.)**

- Elision is called **gradation** by some and involves the loss of a phoneme in connected

speech. This tends to happen in unstressed syllables and, in a sense, elision is a

simplification or an economy made in rapid colloquial speech. In short, in natural

conversation, we tend to glide over weak forms and 'lose' some of them. As a result,

learners of English need to be made aware of it more for their ability to understand native speakers' rapid speech than for their own speech production.

7.5 OMISSION

- The removal of an appetite stimulus after a response, leading to a decrease in behavior. Negative punishment may also be referred to as omission training.
- Omission training – reinforcement is provided when an undesirable behavior is withheld.
- Difference between Positive and Negative Reinforcement:

<u>Types of Negative Punishment</u>

- ○ Response cost – an undesirable behavior results in withdrawal of reward or failure to attain reward.

- Example: loss of privileges

  ○ Time-out – a period of time during which reinforcement is unavailable.

    - Example: being sent to room after misbehaving.

Does Punishment Work?

○ Skinner showed that punishment only temporarily suppresses behavior.
○ More recent studies show that it can permanently suppress behavior under some conditions.
○ Under other conditions it has no effect or only temporarily works.

Severity of Punishment

○ Mild punishment doesn't work.

    - Example: Drunk drivers do it again.
    - With mild punishment, any suppression is short-lived.

○ The more severe the punishment, the longer it works.

    - Example: sale of cigarettes to minors.
    - Must be severe to accomplish permanent behavior change.

Consistency of Punishment

○ Punishment must be consistently administered.

    - Odds of a drunk driver being caught are 1 in 2000.
    - Suppression increases as the frequency of punishment increases.
    - Delinquent boys more likely to have parents who are inconsistent in their discipline.

Delay of Punishment

  ○ Punishment must be immediate in order to be effective.

- Long delay between arrest and trial for drunk drivers.

Drawbacks to Using Punishment

- Pain-induced aggression – pain elicits anger which may motivate aggressive behavior.
- An impulsive act energized by emotional arousal, not avoidance.
- Suppressive effects may generalize from an undesirable behavior to other desirable behaviors.
- Punishment may not generalize to similar undesirable behaviors.
- The person may not recognize the contingency between the behavior and the punishment.
- Modeling of aggression – children may imitate a parent's aggressive acts through observational learning.

7.5 CONSONANT CLUSTERS

A consonant cluster is a group or sequence of consonants that appear together in a syllable without a vowel between them.

In English consonants are found to be clustered in word initial, medial and word final positions. The consonant clusters/ sequence belonging to a single syllable are known as **intra syllabic clusters** whereas the consonant clusters belonging to two different syllables in a single word are known as **inter-syllabic clusters.** Thus, in linguistics, a consonant cluster also known as consonant blend is a group of consonants which have no intervening vowels in between them.

The maximum possibility of consonant cluster is three consonants in the beginning and four in final position.

- Some examples:
  Tray – /tr/ are clustered in word initially in a single syllable. Thus it is intra syllabic cluster.
  Doctor-/kt/ are clustered word medially in two different syllable. Thus it is a inter syllabic cluster
  Apt-/pt/ are clustered word finally but in a single syllable.

7.5.1 Word Initial Clusters

If consonants are sequenced word initially, the cluster is known as word initial cluster.

a) CC cluster: It also has two subtypes. They are:

One of /p,t,k,b,d,g,m,n,l,α, f, v, h, l/ + one of /l, r, w, j/. as for example: play, prey,

  /s/ + one of /p, t , k, f, m, n, l , w, j/. As for example, speak, sky, stick, snail, swim, Shrine, snakes, sticks, sphere, stair, skeet, slope, snow, etc.

b) CCC Cluster: In the word initial position three consonants occur together.

  The structure of this cluster is the following:

/s/ + one of /p, t, k/ + one of /l, r, w, j/. As for example,

Splash, Spring, Strong, Stupid, Screen, Square, Spurious, Screw, Skewer,

7.5.2 Word Final Clusters

  The sequence of consonants in the final position of a word is called word final position consonant cluster. The following types of word final consonant clusters can be found:

a) – CC Cluster: As for example, Slept, taps, caps, depth, jobs, robbed, books, looks, bags, watched, draft, craft, graphs, etc.

b) – CCC cluster: As for example, Pushed, gasp, ask, test, restCamp, ramp, warmth, terms, rent, dent, bench, pens, gulp, bulb, film, gold, sold, told, solve, etc.

c) – CCCC Cluster: As for example, Milked, tempt, arranged, whilst, jumps, months, acts, amongst, texts, sixths, prompts, etc.

7.5.3 Word Medial Clusters

The cluster of consonants in the middle position of the word is called word middle consonant cluster. There are two types of word medial consonant clusters. They are:

a) Intra-syllabic consonant cluster: The sequence of consonants in the word medial position which belong to the same syllable is called intra-syllabic cluster. As for example, camping, reply, windy, extra, etc.

b) Inter-syllabic cluster: If the consonant belonging to different syllables occurs together, the cluster formed is called inter-syllabic cluster. As for example,

movement /vm/,

description /skr/

import /mp/

blackboard /kb/

extra /kstr/

Some more examples of consonant clusters:

a) Nasal + stop – camp, bend, stamp, etc.

b) Nasal + fricative – length, warmth, terms, kings, etc.

c) Stop + stop – packed, begged, kept, tract, etc.

d) Stop + nasal – written, bitten, certain, etc.

e) Stop + lateral – middle, cattle, bottle, huddle, etc.

f) Nasal + affricate – change, bench, lunch, etc.

g) Fricative + stop – best, test, ask, draft, etc.

h) Lateral + fricative – health, wealth, solve, etc.

VIII
STUDENT MANAGEMENT

Objective:

Managing your students isn't always easy. Capturing their attention, holding their interest, and involving them to reach the desired results in training our challenging to say the least. Not to mention those who simply rebel or have disciplinary problems.

How to manage all this so your sessions run smoothly? We'll discover the possibilities in this module.

Topics:

ax.   Student management techniques
ax.   How to maintain discipline
ax.   Mentoring

Many trainers make the mistake of feeling they should give students freedom to behave in their own way, or they may not be able to develop a positive relationship if they are strict. Here are some helpful techniques to manage your students without sacrificing your rapport with them.

1.   **Focusing**

The focusing technique means that you will demand your students' attention before you begin. It means that you will wait until everyone has settled down. Experienced trainers know that silence on their part is very effective. They will punctuate their waiting by extending it 3 to 5 seconds after the classroom is completely quiet. Then they begin their lesson using a quieter voice than normal.

2. Direct Instruction

The technique of direct instruction is to begin each class by telling the students exactly what will be happening. The trainer outlines what he and the students will be doing this period.

3. Monitoring

The key to this principle is to circulate. Get up and get around the room. While your students are working, make the rounds. Check on their progress. Provide individualized instruction as needed. Don't interrupt the class or try to make general announcements unless you notice that several students have difficulty with the same thing. Your students will appreciate your personal and positive attention.

4. Modeling

"Values are caught, not taught." Trainers who are courteous, prompt, enthusiastic, in control, patient and organized provide examples for their students through their own behavior. The "do as I say, not as I do" trainers send mixed messages that confuse students and invite misbehavior.

5. Non-Verbal Cuing

You need not always speak to get your point across. Non-verbal cues like facial expressions, body posture and hand signals can be used effectively. Care should be given in choosing the types of cues you use in your classroom. Some cues might need to be explained as to what you want the students to do when you use them.

6. Low-Profile Intervention

Most trainer-student conflicts can be avoided when the trainer's intervention is quiet and calm. An effective trainer will take care that the students is not rewarded for misbehavior by becoming the focus of attention. He anticipates problems before they occur. His approach to a misbehaving student is inconspicuous. Others in the class are not distracted.

7. Assertive Discipline

This is traditional limit setting authoritarianism. When executed effectively it will include a good mix of praise with discipline. The trainer is the boss and no student has the right to interfere with the learning of any other student. Clear rules are laid out and consistently enforced.

8. Humanistic "I" Messages

These "I" messages are expressions of our feelings. Here we structure these messages in three parts. First, include a description of the student's behavior. "When you talk while I talk..." Second, relate this behavior has on the training. "...I have to stop my teaching..." And third, let the student know the feeling that it generates in the trainer. "...which frustrates me."

However, we must take care while utilizing this technique. Here's an example of how it can go too far: A trainer, distracted by a student who was constantly talking while he tried to teach, once made this powerful expression of feelings: "I cannot imagine what I have done to you that I do not deserve the respect from you that I get from the others in this class. I feel as though I have somehow offended you and now you are unwilling to show me respect." The student did not talk during his lectures again for many weeks.

9. Positive Discipline

Use classroom rules that describe the behavior you want instead of listing things the students cannot do. Instead of "no ringing of cell phones in class", use "please answer calls after class." Instead of "don't be late to class," use "please be on time." Instead of "don't say it that way," use "please say it this way." Refer to your rules as expectations. Let your students know this is how you except them to behave in your classroom.

Make ample use of praise. When you see good behavior, acknowledge it. This can be done verbally, of course, but it doesn't have to be. A nod, a smile or a "thumbs up" will reinforce the behavior just as well.

10. **Listen**

Listen to your students' feedback. The training is for them and their benefit. If they would like to learn in a different way or change the topic or have a suggestion, please listen to them. Never make the mistake that your lesson plans are etched in stone and you know what's best - you're the trainer, they're the student. Students' suggestions are insights as to how to make your training more effective. Always be open to their negative feedback along with the good.

Student Management - Discipline

Also, remember to let them talk about things outside the parameters of the training agenda. It's good if they open up about their personal life a bit. Let them also talk among themselves when time permits. Not all chatter and banter is a nuisance. You can gain valuable insight into your training effectiveness and do a gap analysis. Allowing as many comfortable opportunities for them to speak English is they key.

Discipline Issues

Students provide most of of the challenges, fulfillment, and joy of teaching, as well as many of its frustrations. They are an invaluable source of friendship and local information for those teachers working away from home, and they bring a fund of knowledge and opinions on a great variety of subjects into the classroom.

No two students and two classes are alike. Be prepared for a language topic or activity, which works with one group to be a complete flop with another.

Students who pose problems belong to three categories:

1. **Weak students** who can be a burden to the class, and often become demotivated.
2. **Strong students** make progress at a more rapid pace than the rest of the class, and need challenging tasks to engage their attention.
3. **Difficult students** can jeopardize everyone's progress by disrupting class. With experience you will spot and deal with these problems effectively but, before that, do your best, and be aware that these are problems even

the best teacher has to face.

Causes of Discipline Problems in class:

ax.   A gap in a lesson (bad planning,, an activity loses momentum; a piece of equipment fails to work)
ax.   Unclear instructions (they don't know what to do, they don't start and attention wanders)
ax.   Trainer doesn't set boundaries
ax.   Lack of trainer's attention
ax.   Work is too easy or too challenging
ax.   Not focusing on learner styles or employing the right methodology/tools

Be wary of the following traps that a trainer can fall into while trying to gain control of a classroom:

ax.   Threats
ax.   Public humiliation
ax.   Shouting back at them
ax.   Punishing the whole class for the behavior of a few

Final Tips on How to Manage your Students

· **Establish class conventions from the very beginning**

These include punctuality, the use of target language only, and meeting assignments allotted. It is much easier to be firm about these things at the start and loosen up later.

· **Impose your presence**

This does not mean that you try to act domineering. Use your physical presence and your speaking style to manage the room.

· **Be well prepared**

Set the agenda and have a plan, which you all follow. don't always ask them what they would like to do or what they want to talk about.

- **Allow for a certain amount of noise**

In India, a quiet classroom is normally considered a disciplined classroom where learning is taking place. This is evidently at odds with your role, which is to maximize students experiential learning opportunities, with reasonable noise levels. Clearly, a class that is in control is not always quiet and a quiet class with the teacher doing all the talking is not necessarily a good learning environment.

Student Management: Mentoring

As we've already learned, one of the hats a trainer wears is a friend and mentor. Wearing this hat actually serves as a very effective tool to managing your students. Maintaining a good rapport with authority is the right balance to strike. Being a good mentor is the key.

An effective mentoring relationship passes through several development phases. Early on, a mentor recognizes a student's unique qualities and believes the student deserves special coaching. In turn, this recognition inspires the student, who seeks to benefit from the mentor's support, skills and wisdom.

Mentorship is far more than a conversation about your students' goals or counseling them on success. It is the mentor's continuous engagement in a student's growth and the ongoing support and encouragement of students' endeavors.

It is important to remember that effective mentoring, like wisdom itself, is multidimensional. The best mentors adjust their multiple roles to meet different students' needs. While there is no single formula for good mentoring, it is important that you know that **mentoring focuses on the human relationships, commitments and resources that help students find success and fulfillment in their skill development and professional pursuits.**

Here are some principles we can follow to be an effective mentor to our students.

- Engage students in ongoing conversations
- Show that you care about their improvement
- Provide constructive and supportive feedback
- Provide encouragement
- Foster alternative/further learning opportunities
- Look out students' interests

- Treat students with respect
- Provide a personal touch

SUMMARY

In conclusion, this book has aimed to provide a comprehensive guide for aspiring and current trainers, equipping them with the essential knowledge and skills required to excel in their roles. By exploring the multifaceted nature of being a trainer, we have delved into various aspects that contribute to professional growth and effective training delivery.

Key Takeaways:

Becoming A Professional Trainer:
We began with an introduction to the foundational qualities and goals of a professional trainer, emphasizing the importance of adhering to established standards and continuously striving for excellence.

The Five Hats of a Trainer:
We examined the diverse roles trainers must adopt, from being a professional and a medium of knowledge, to acting as a facilitator, teacher, and mentor. Each role requires a unique set of skills and approaches to effectively engage and support learners.

Activities Suited to Learning Styles:
Understanding and catering to different learning styles is crucial for maximizing the impact of training sessions. We discussed various activities that align with specific learning preferences, ensuring that all participants can benefit from the training.

Interview of a Trainer:
Insights from experienced trainers highlighted effective training methodologies, the importance of utilizing diverse learning tools, and strategies for handling discipline, thereby enriching our understanding of best practices in training delivery.

Training Needs Analysis (TNA):
We explored the process of conducting a thorough TNA to identify training requirements and gather feedback, which is essential for designing relevant and impactful training programs.

Lesson Plan on Confidence:
A detailed lesson plan on building confidence demonstrated how structured and well-planned sessions can foster essential skills in learners.

Voice and Accent:

The chapter on voice and accent covered critical aspects of phonology, blending, segmentation, and other elements that contribute to clear and effective communication, which is a vital skill for any trainer.

Student Management:

Effective student management techniques were discussed to help trainers create a positive and productive learning environment.

Final Thoughts:

Moving Forward:

As you move forward in your journey as a trainer, remember that continuous learning and adaptability are key. The landscape of training and development is ever-evolving, and staying updated with the latest trends and methodologies will help you remain relevant and effective.

Engage with your peers, seek feedback, and reflect on your experiences to identify areas for improvement. By doing so, you will not only enhance your own skills but also significantly contribute to the growth and development of your learners.

Training is not just about imparting knowledge; it is about inspiring and empowering others to achieve their potential. As a trainer, you have the opportunity to make a profound impact on the lives of individuals and the success of organizations. Embrace this responsibility with passion and dedication, and you will undoubtedly leave a lasting legacy in the field of training and development.

Thank you for embarking on this journey with me. I wish you all the best in your endeavors as a professional trainer.

Thank You

This book would not have been possible without the support and guidance of numerous individuals and organizations. Firstly, I would like to extend my heartfelt gratitude to my mentors and colleagues who have been instrumental in shaping my career as a professional trainer. Their insights and encouragement have been invaluable.

Special thanks to the dedicated team of editors and reviewers whose meticulous attention to detail and constructive feedback have greatly enhanced the quality of this work. I am also grateful to the many trainers and educators who shared their experiences and knowledge, enriching the content of this book.

REFERENCES

Brown, H. D. (2007). Principles of Language Learning and Teaching. Pearson Education.

Gardner, H. (1983). Frames of Mind: The Theory of Multiple Intelligences. Basic Books.

Knowles, M. S., Holton, E. F., & Swanson, R. A. (2015). The Adult Learner: The Definitive Classic in Adult Education and Human Resource Development. Routledge.

Kolb, D. A. (1984). Experiential Learning: Experience as the Source of Learning and Development. Prentice-Hall.

Merriam, S. B., & Bierema, L. L. (2013). Adult Learning: Linking Theory and Practice. Jossey-Bass.

www.ingramcontent.com/pod-product-compliance
Lightning Source LLC
Chambersburg PA
CBHW041646150726

48005CB00015BA/2418